AUTHOR
THROP, J.

CLASS
TS61

TITLE
Poems from "Lancashire life"

606

Poems from Lancashire Life

by
Jonty Throp

Dalesman Books
1987

The Dalesman Publishing Company Ltd.,
Clapham, Lancaster, LA2 8EB.
First published 1987
© Joseph Thorpe, 1987
Illustrations © Opax Publishing Ltd. 1985
© A. McWhirter, 1987
ISBN: 0 85206 909 X

"Jonty Throp" is the name under which the dialect poems in this book were originally published in *Lancashire Life.* It is the pen-name of Joseph Thorpe, treasurer of the Lancashire Dialect Society.

Born in Leigh in 1914, Joseph Thorpe stems from real Lancashire parentage — his father was a tub fettler and his mother a four-loom weaver. Educated at Leigh Grammar School, he went to Manchester University where he graduated with a first-class honours degree in mathematics — and the loss of his "Lanky" tongue. After a career with Customs and Excise, he retired in 1979 and a year later wrote the first of many "Lanky dialect" poems reflecting what he admits is a slightly wicked sense of humour.

Printed by Fretwell & Cox Limited,
Goulbourne Street, Keighley, West Yorkshire BD21 1PZ.

Contents

Foreword

The best poetry — indeed, the best writing of any discipline — is that produced because the author "couldn't help it": a labour of love, born of creative compulsion.

Joseph Thorpe can't help it. Such was his output in my *Lancashire Life* days that I warned him he was courting a kind of immortality. Only one of his poems could be accommodated each month, and they were queueing up in numbers suggesting that those towards the end of the line were destined for posthumous publication. Was there life after death? Yes — if you were Joseph Thorpe, your poems would go marching on.

Now, thanks to their assembly between book covers, those poems gathered here will doubtless outlive their author — still happily with us. I am delighted to see them thus preserved, deservedly exhumed from their graveyard of magazine back-numbers.

What prompted me to print them, month after month, over several years? No, it wasn't because their author had met the late, lamented dialect writer T. Thompson, an encounter which in Lancashire eyes comes close to touching Shakespeare's hem. To see why Joseph Thorpe's poems became a regular feature of *Lancashire Life,* you need do only one thing: read them.

William Amos
Editor, *Lancashire Life,* 1970–85

A. McWhirter

Playgreawnds

Th'owd 'eawse Ah were born in
'Ad flagstones waw to waw,
Three up, three deawn un' t'coal'ole,
Un' th'ash-pit, t'petty un' aw.

O't'other side o'th'ash-pit
Were t'back wheer t'weshin' were dried.
It med us a champion playgreawnd —
It mun 'a bin fifty foot wide!

For 'eawrs on eend Ah played theer
When Ah were nobbut a lad
Ut tick un' punch un' thruss-weight
Un' piggy un' duck un' swadd.

Wi' a tally-pow fo't' swaarm up
Un' umpteen waws fo't' climb
We ne'er geet tired o'playin';
We 'ad a reet beltin' time.

There wuz other playgreawnds t'go to
If we geet dischuffed wi't'back,
'Cause owt'll meck a playgreawnd
If yo'n nobbut getten t'knack.

There wuz sidin's full o'waggons,
Un' lodges, flashes un' brucks.
There wuz brick 'ills, saw-mills, scrapyards
Un' a two-three pits wi' rucks.

There were t'cut wi' its turnin' bridges;
There were Lilford Park wi' its wood.
There were varnear nowt we were short on;
I reckon nob'dy 'ad it so good.

We ned no Adventure Playgreawnds,
Me un' mi Abbey Street mates.
We wuz 'appy uz pigs i' pig-muck
Un' we ne'er ned a penny fro't'rates.

7

Exile

When I first came to Warrington
I couldn't believe my ears,
For no-one spoke the dialect
I'd loved for forty years.

Wherever I went wandering,
In Penketh or Great Sankey,
In Woolston or in Martinscroft,
I heard more Scouse than Lanky.

I learned to my astonishment
In Poulton-with-Fearnhead,
Like Latin was in Italy,
The dialect was dead.

I looked for Lanky high and low
From Culcheth through to Cuerdley
And found some gradely folk in Croft
Still spoke it self-assuredly.

And just a few in Rixton too,
And Winwick and Burtonwood,
But nowhere else in Warrington
Was Lanky understood.

I've now lived here for thirty year —
That's nearly half my life —
With Know-No-Lanky progeny
And Knows-No-Lanky wife.

I've learned by heart the Lanky verse
Which fills my bedside shelf
But only heard the spoken word
When talking to myself.

To me it's still incredible,
So inexplicably queer,
That Leigh where I learned Lanky lies
A mere nine miles from here!

Computermania

I'm sick of this ridiculous fuss
About the electric abacus;
Because if there's a power cut
The entire nation does its nut,
And even Maths undergrads can't contrive
To add three and two and arrive at five.

I learned when young to calculate
With pencil screeching on a slate,
But nowadays, of course, instead
I work it all out in my head.
It's a pity slates are out of date
When millons are innumerate.

Disbelief

What I heard on my radio
I thought was rather rum.
What Irishman would want to write
About a cockney bum?

I heard the man enunciate
With extraordinary care:
"And now that lovely Irish tune:
The London derrière."

No Joke

Some friend had on my parcel penned:
"Important photos do not bend."
Some foe had added: "Yes they do!"
The so-and-so had proved it too.

Yon Mon

'E's plagued me neaw for fifty year,
Yon mon!
'E stinks th'eawse eawt wi' 'is bacca and beer,
Yon mon!
'E goes o't' batter beawt teckin' 'is key
Then wakkens me up at 'afe past three,
'E spends mooar time wi' 'is pigeons than me,
Yon mon!

'E's allus been a Wanderer's fan,
Yon mon!
'E's backed aw th'orses as also ran,
Yon mon!
When they won 'e'd treat me like a queen,
But when they geet byitten 'e geet reet mean.
'E'd come womm kettled and black my e'en,
Yon mon!

'E's allus kept me short o' brass,
Yon mon!
'E wouldn't do beawt 'is pipe or 'is glass,
Yon mon!
When 'e were on t'dole, on t'club or on strike
We were thar 'ard up I often 'ad a skrike,
But would 'e gi' o'er suppin'? Would 'e 'eck as like,
Yon mon!

'E wain't lift a finger t'elp i'th'eawse,
Yon mon!
'E says 'e's a mon and nor a flippin' meawse,
Yon mon!
'E wain't side t'pots, 'e wain't wesh up,
'E wain't bile t'kettle when 'e wannts summat t'sup,
'E wain't sterr 'is tay when I've sugared 'is cup,
Yon mon!

'E ne'er e'er tecks me eawt at aw,
Yon mon!
I 'ave t'stop a-womm and stare at t'waw,
Yon mon!
At t'Wakes we ne'er goo onnywheer,
'E says there's nowheer as nice as 'ere,
And 'e wain't sup nowt but Bowton beer,
Yon mon!

'E's ne'er done nowt as 'e owt to 'a' done,
Yon mon!
I've cawed 'im aw t'names under t'sun,
Yon mon!
'E's allus led me a reet owd jig,
'E's not fit live wi' till 'e's 'ad enoof t'swig,
Bur I wouldn't swop 'im for a gowd pig,
Yon mon!

Street Accents

Ah cawn't stond *Coronation Street*
When th'actors don't get th'accent reet.
Some on 'um if Ah'm noan mistook
Favver they'n learnt it eawt uv a book.

Un' some uz come fro' God knows wheer
Ne'er try fo't' talk like folk reawnd 'ere.
It's stupid Bert un' Ivy's lad
Not speighkin' like 'is Mam un' Dad.

Yon nits uz ne'er get th'accent reet
Are speighlin' *Coronation Street*.
Why cawn't t'daft foo's uz run TV
Pick folk uz talk like me un' thee?

Rhyme without Reason

Writing poems for the swanky
Frightens folk who think in Lanky.
I get collywobbly bowels
Rhyming non-North-Country vowels.

Used to rhyming shut with foot
I'm never sure what words to put.
Dithering over hath and bath
I take the least resistant path.

I have to strain my brain for days
To frame a phrase devoid of A's
And lest it should confuse my Muse
The phrase I choose must have no U's.

So as such problems cease to be
If all the verse one writes is free
I think from rhyming I'll retire
And be a gratis versifier.

Mardypot

When Dad poo'd eawt 'is pouch un' pipe
Mam sut theer wi' a face like tripe.
'Er met 'a' purr 'im off 'is smook
If 'e'd 'a' getten t'guts fo't'look.

A gradely mardypot were Dad;
'E ne'er could bear fo't see Mam sad.
'Er 'ated t'stink o'Navy Cut
So 'e allus smooked wi' booath e'en shut.

Lanky Hanky Panky

'T'were just afther t'last warr 'ad eended
Eawr Seth went un' flit fro' Chowbent.
'E never were 'appy wi' Folkestone:
They couldn't talk proper i' Kent.

'E allus come womm abeawt Christmas
Wi' 'is missis, a Leighther cawed Peg,
Un' one year 'e geet this daft notion:
'E wannted t'poo t'ticket mon's leg.

'E sheawted through t'daft little windo':
"Gi' us two chep returns to Chowbent!"
Reckonin' uz nob'dy i' Folkestone
'Ould know worr it were uz e' meant.

But this ticket mon were a Keaw-Yed
Uz 'ad played Wingates' second trombone,
So 'e axed: "Dost wannt Atherton Central
Or is it 'Owe Bridge or Bag Loan?"

Recitations

They said uz a mon uz writes po'try's a puff.
(That's posh name fer one o' them theer.)
And nobbut a nancy owt t'fancy yon stuff —
A gradely mon's 'obby is beer.

But neaw Ah've bin towd Ah'm committin' no crime
Wi mi odd bits o' Lankyfied writin':
There's nowt wrung wi' meckin' up pieces uz rhyme
So lung uz they're wrote fer recitin'.

Harry Barker 1982

Th'Avvy Lake

I 'ad some fun an' no mistake
When I used t'fish i'th'Avvy Lake
Back i'Nineteen Twenty-odd
Wi' nobbut an owd brush stale for a rod,
An' a bit o' streng an' a pin as I'd bent
An' an empty jam jar, off we went,
Teckin' eawr butties an' a bottle o' pop
An' braggin' abeawt 'eaw monny we'd cop.

Breakfast done I went o't'lavvy
Then deawn t'street an' into th'Avvy
Teckin' t'road we allus took
Over t'train lines then o'er t'brook.
'Owdin' tight to t'Bruno tin
I'd fotched fo't' put my wazzums in,
I'd climb o'er t'rails o't'lotment plot
Wheer I knowed they could be got.

When I thowt I'd getten enough
I'd run to t'lake fo't'do my stuff.
I'd skewer a wazzum on my pin,
Wetch 'im wiggle then duck 'im in,
'Opin' a jacksharp or a pike
'Ould wannt 'im for their breakfast, like.
There wuz allus theawsands close to t'shore —
Th'Avvy Lake 'ad fish galore.

So if yo'd learnt fo't' shut yo'r gob
Coppin' fish were a bobby's job.
We'd fish until we 'ad fo't' stop
Because eawr jars wuz full to t'top.
So, pop aw supped an' butties etten,
We keawnted up 'eaw monny we'd getten.
I allus went womm full o' glee —
Nob'dy copped as monny as me.

⇩

T'past fifty year I've bin away
Burr 'appenin' t'be i'Leighth t'other day
I went up th'Avvy for owd times' sake
Burr I couldn't find no Avvy Lake.
I walked varnear to Wood Eend Pit
Burr I ne'er seed no sign of it,
Nor t'train lines noather nor t'lotment plot,
Someb'dy 'ad shifted t'bloomin' lot.

'Eawses an' 'eawses, row on row,
Covered aw wheer I used fo't'go.
An' I couldn't 'elp thinkin' o't'fun we'd 'ad
Aw reawnd theer when I were a lad.
I looked at t'place wheer t'lake 'ad been
An' I couldn't stop t'tears wellin' up i' my e'en
Fo't'think as t'planners 'ad come one day
An' tecken t'best part o' my life away.

Gradely Things

Brass met beigh thi varnear owt
But gradely things con ne'er be bowt;
Like findin' childer love thee 'cause
Theaw even loves 'um when they're nowt.

Like seein' tears well i' t'wife's e'en
When 'er thowt theaw were past romance
Fo't find theaw's spent thi bacca brass
On beighin' summat daft 'er wannts.

Ah've ne'er 'ad brass fo't chuck abeawt;
Ah reckon Ah've bin missin' nowt
Sin Ah've 'ad mooer ner Ah disarve
O' t'gradely things uz cawn't be bowt.

Lanky Geoggy

Folk get lost i'Lankasheer
Tryin' t'get from 'ere to theer;
It's t'same as when yo'n bin abroad,
Nowheer's wrote t'same road it's cawed.

Tyldesley's Bongs and Atherton's Bent,
Glazebury's wrote when Burry Lone's meant,
Leigh is Leighth wheer it's bin known
For folk t'caw 'Ilton Park Kecka Lone.

It's a reet doolally 'eaw-de-yo-do,
Liverpool's t'Poo, so's Blackpool too,
Lamberhead's Lomra when it comes to Greens,
Chequerbent's allus Four Lone Eends.

Yo' con waste t'best part o' th'afternoon
When t'sign says Poulton-le-Fylde, not Poon.
An' some folks 'ave bin known fo' t'clem
Skennin' reawnd Skelmersdale seechin' for Skem.

It sometimes varnear gets yo' deawn,
Bolton's Bowton or t'Trotters' Teawn,
Westhoughton's 'Owfen or Keaw Yed City
An' what they caw Ramsbottom's norra bit pretty.

Yo' don't 'afe feel a proper mutt
When yo' find t'Ship Canal's what they aw caw t'Cut,
An' nobbut a clever-clogs knows for sure
When'e's getten t'Ainsworth 'e's at Cocky Moor.

So if yo're wanntin' t'go to Bent
An' yo' don't wannt t'wish yo'd never went
Meck sure afooer yo' gerr i' t'car
Yo'n fun' eawt what t'reet road-signs are.

Lancashire Rules O.K.

To work in Warrington I came
And everyone said: "What a shame!
You have not got the right address —
You live in Lancs and not in Ches."

They said I might as well be dead
As live in Poulton-with-Fearnhead
For only imbeciles and cranks
Elected to reside in Lancs.

But, being Lanky born and bred,
I'd chosen Poulton-with-Fearnhead
So I could keep a Lancs address
I really didn't fancy Ches.

I wouldn't live there at any price
So I declined their kind advice.
But with re-organisational pranks
My address is Ches instead of Lancs.

No thanks to Government Thinking Tanks,
Who thought they'd brought me out of Lancs,
Their manoeuvres didn't move me and mine
Out of the County Palatine.

God bless our gracious royal duke
Who lets Lancastrians off the hook
To cock a snook at mountebanks
Who tried to kick us out of Lancs.

Antithesis

Everyone likes Betty.
No-one cares for Kitty.
Kitty's pretty bloody.
Betty's bloody pretty.

Song of the Ribblethorpe Weavers

Shuttles racing right and left,
Interlacing warp and weft,
Thrusting, threading weft through warp,
Weaving twill in Ribblethorpe.
Weaving twill, weaving twill, weaving twill in Ribblethorpe.

We half-timers, mee-maw mimers,
Wanting to weave till we were dead,
Prattled while our shuttles rattled,
Lip-read words unheard, unsaid.
Lip-read words, lip-read words, lip-read words unheard, unsaid.

Looms that clattered while we chattered
Made a mint for men who mattered;
Then a terrible calamity struck:
Ribblethorpe Mill ran out of luck.
Ribblethorpe Mill, Ribblethorpe Mill, Ribblethorpe Mill ran out
of luck.

Men with a plan thought catch-catch-can
Could match the judo of Japan,
Lost the fight they fought for cotton;
Ribblethorpe twill was soon forgotten.
Ribblethorpe twill, Ribblethorpe twill, Ribblethorpe twill was
soon forgotten.

We were cheerful, learning weaving,
Weaving twill with warp and weft;
We were tearful leaving weaving,
We were grieving when we left.
We were grieving, we were grieving, we were grieving when
we left.

But though the old mill looks bereft
And long ago the last loom left,
We, the unwanted, long since dead,
Still weave twill in the haunted shed.
Still weave twill, still weave twill, still weave twill in the
haunted shed.

Let us *not* praise Famous Men

The English are
Masters of understatement,
A practice pretty prevalent
In proverbially proud Preston
And probably present in
Practically every prominent part
Of the Palatinate.

A typical example is:
"I moan't grumble."
Which may be freely
Translated as:
"I am simply bursting
With good health and
Absolutely bubbling over
With ebullience."

The practice is
Particularly pernicious
When praise appears appropriate.

It is preposterous
To disparage
A perfect performance
By a perfunctory:
"I've 'eerd wuss."
And nothing short of sinful
To say of something
Simply superb:
"It weren't bad."

Only Palatine people
Can properly appreciate
The apparent paradox
Of paying compliments
By damning
With faint praise.

Amos Malaprop

When Amos murdered 'is owd mon
I couldn't fathom why.
I knowed as 'e were pots for rags
Bur 'e wouldn't 'urt a fly.

'E towd 'um why 'e'd kilt th'owd lad
At t'cop-shop wheer they'd brung 'im:
'''E med me 'is Executor
So I geet t'clooas line an' 'ung 'im!''

Gawmin' Lanky

Yon Welchmon what wed t'wench next dooer
It favvers cawn't gawm Lanky.
'E's varneer druv 'is wife up t'waw —
'Er's not 'afe getten cranky.
Sin t'waw's that thin we'n 'eeard 'er sheawt:
"What med me wed a ninny?
Why 'asta bin un browt me brat?
Ah axed thee t'fotch mi pinny!"

'Er'd getten Ivor that dischuffed
Bi sayin' 'e were dim,
Ah thowt Ah owt sort summat eawt
Fert 'elp booath 'er un 'im.
Ah axed mi-sel wor Ah'd wannt t'know
If Ah wuz in 'is shoes
Un tried t'explain a two-three words
Uz t'folk reawnd 'ere aw use.

Ah wrote uz beawt means getten noan,
Un fund is t'same uz feawnd,
Uz clemmed means t'gut thinks t'throttle's cut;
No cop means nowt a peawnd.
A-swint is same uz like skew-wiff,
A moggie's owt what's wick,
A bun i'th'oon means get wed soon,
Up t'stick means get wed quick.

A shive's fer meckin' butties wi',
Un jackbit's t'same uz snap;
Thi lugs is ayther side thi een
Un t'gob is t'same uz t'trap.
It's tipplin' means it's teemin' deawn
Un t'jawm's at t'side o't'dooer
Un guzzlin's sooart o'gollopin'
But luggin's poo'in' yure.

Thi chops is what theaw mee-maws wi';
Dobbers un alleys is merps;
Left-footer's worr a red-neck's cawed
Un riftin's belkin' burps.
'Avin' a decko's 'avin' a sken,
Airyated's proper eggy,
Fert parr or purr's what clugs is fer
Un kibbo's t'same uz keggy.

Witchert's geet thi feet reet weet
Un tah-tah's someb'dy mard;
A snotrag's wor a nooas-clout's cawed
Un t'petty's what's deawn t'yard.
What Keaw-Yeds met caw livin' o'er t'broosh
In Leighth's cawed livin' tally
Un reet pow-fagged means proper shagged
But reet reawned t'twist's doolally.

'Is wife sez 'e's no nearer neaw,
It's still aw double-dutch;
Though aw Ah writ's uz plain uz plain
To 'im it's clear uz slutch.
'Eaw con a mon be numb uz yon?
Ah reckon 'e's a skiver
Sin nowt a one-year-owd con gawm
Owt be too 'ard for Ivor.

Idle Jack

Eawr Jack used t'graft fer t'Wayter Booard
But ne'er seed brucks ner oceans;
'E cawed 'is-sel a chemist but
Ne'er med up no potions.

'E warked i't'lab at t'Sewerage Farm
So folk geet reet quare notions —
They reckoned 'e ne'er knowed what wark were,
'E nobbut went through t'motions.

T'Lanky Twang

Ah cawn't get th'ang
O't' Lanky twang;
'Appen Ah'm numb uz a brick,
Burr Ah 'ave t'admit
It's getten me b'yit;
It's gerrin' on mi wick.
'Cos Ah cawn't see 'eaw
If yo' caw cow keaw
Uz brow's not breaw it's broo;
Un' if no's now
Go owt t'bi gow
So why do yo aw say goo?

No met bi now
Burr a po's nor a pow
'Cos a pow is wot yo' caw a pole
Un' though bowl's bow
A foal's norr a fow
Un' cow's not wot yo' caw coal.
First is fust
But thirst's not thust
Un' burst's ayther bust or brast.
Bird is brid
But third's not thrid
Un' dirt's not drit it's nast.

Gape is gawp
Un' scrape is scrawp
But Cawp's not cape it's a shop.
A sack's a seck
Burr a rack's norr a wreck
Un' a tec's norr a tack it's a cop.
Old is owd
Un' gold is gowd
But powed means thi yure's bin cut.
Gave is gi'ed
But grave's not grid
Un' rid's not rave it's getten shut.

Peawnd means pound
Un' greawnd means ground
Un' found's ayther fund or feawnd.
If fotch means fetch
Why is watch wetch?
Why is it t'other road reawnd?
'Appen Ah'm dense
Un' Ah cawn't see sense
But they met uz weel talk Greek
'Cos it's not much 'elp
If they caw cheek chelp
If they don't say whelp for week.

Ah'll ne'er get th'ang
O't'Lanky twang
Burr it's noan fer't'wannt o' axin'.
There's norr a college
Getten t'knowledge —
They'd raither gab Anglo-Saxin.
But nob'dy knowed
If there were a reet road
O'learnin' 'eaw t'talk Lanky.
If there's no rules
Yo cawn't 'ave schools
So it favvers Ah'll 'ave t'talk swanky.

Numb-yed

Ah were such a foo ut skoo
Uz t'teighcher once said: "Sithee!
Ah know theaw's allus 'ad meck do
Wi' t'bit o' brain God gi' thi.
But wi' this sum theaw's bin that numb
Ah reckon theaw's left thi brain a-wumm.
Morn mornin' when it's time fert come
Think on un fotch it wi' thi."

Smookin'

Mi faither's main 'obby were smookin'.
'E'd allus a pipe in 'is gob
Un' Mam favvered t'allus t'be chunnerin'
Abeawt aw t'brunt matchstalks reawnd th'ob.

When 'er geet proper mangy 'er'd tell 'im
'E thowt mooer o't'pipe than 'is wife.
Ah couldn't stond seein' Mam skrikin'
Un' it put me off smookin' for life.

But sin Ah've bin gerrin' a bit past it
Ah've thowt abeawt nowt but mi dad;
'E lived fo't be o'er ninety-seven —
A gradely good-tempered owd lad.

'E'd allus bin mad abeawt ramblin'
Un' thowt nowt o' traipsin' ten mile.
Bi then 'e could do nowt but shuffle
Un' 'ad ne'er bin through t'dooer for some while.

'E allus like skennin' through t'papper
Fo't' see if 'is skoo-pals 'ad deed.
Bi then we 'ad t'tell 'im who'd snuffed it.
'Is seet geet too bad for 'im t'read.

Burr worr 'e liked best were a natter
Wi 'is owd marrers Abel un' Seth,
But when 'e went deef they stopped comin';
They felt they'd be wastin' their breath.

But noan o' that favvered t'upset 'im —
'E'd ne'er bin a meightherin' type —
'E sut theer i't'cheer lookin' 'appy,
Puffin' away at 'is pipe.

Un' Ah think when Ah'm too owd fo't' do owt
Un' 'appen confined to mi bed
If Ah cawn't smook a pipe t'meck me 'appy
What the 'ell con Ah find t'do i'stead?

T'Gradely Ale Guide

Although Ah'd bin to Blackpoo'
Wheer Ah'd stopped i'digs o't'prom
Until Ah went i'th'army
Ah'd ne'er lived away fro' womm.

Ah'd never bin a boozer
Though Ah'd supped a gill or two
But varnear every gill Ah'd supped
'Ad bin o't'local brew.

So t'neet afore Ah went away
Fo' t' wear a khaki suit
Mi fayther axed mi t'goo wi''im
To t'Pitmon's Institute.

We geet shut of a couple o' quarrts
Afore we went to bed
While Fayther gi'ed mi this advice
Uz stood mi in good stead:

''Worrever camp they send thee to
There'll be a NAAFI theer.
They're noan so bad for char un' a wad
But noan so good for beer.

''So when theaw'rt feelin' thirsty
Un' theaw wannts a change fro' char
Start seechin' for a little pub
Wheer t'landlord serves at t'bar.

''Un' just afore theaw goes inside
Remember fo' t' meck sure
Theaw's tecken note o't'landlord's name
What's written over t'dooer.

''So when 'e axes what theaw wannts
Theaw'll caw 'im bi 'is name
Un' beigh 'im worr 'e allus sups
Un' tell 'im theaw'll 'a't'same.

"For whether pubs is brewery-tied
Or whether pubs is free
What's good enough for landlords
Owt be good enough for thee."

Short Gut

There's no such thing
As too much ale —
There's not enough dark,
There's not enough pale.
I'd drink it morn
To midnight but
I haven't got
Sufficient gut.
There's not much more
Than twenty feet
Of gut between
My mouth and seat,
So I keep hoping
I won't burst,
Coping with a
Thirty foot thirst.

Chuckin' Eawt Time

Ah 'ate pub landlords wi' a stutter,
Detest pub managers uz mutter,
Bur abominate t'words uz aw on um utter:
"An yo lot getten no womms fert gutter!"

Harry Barker

Lanky Limericks

There wuz a pit broo lass fro' Bongs
Uz ett aw 'er jackbit wi' tongs.
When axed why this woz
'Er said: "It's becoz
Ah'm allergic to owt uz 'az prongs."

There wuz a young tackler fro' Bowton
Uz went fer a walk ter West'owton,
But when 'e geet theer
'E said: "There's nowt 'ere."
Un' then beggared off back to Bowton.

A black-puddin' mecker fro' Burry
Went womm wi' a carry-eawt curry.
Next morn 'e said: "Mother,
Ah waint wannt another,
Ah 'ad t'go deawn t'yard in an 'urry."

A reet bobby-dazzler fro' Parr
Poo'ed pints in a St Helens bar;
But t'lads uz med glasses
'Ad ne'er med no passes —
They aw thowt uz Parr wuz too far.

More Lanky Limericks

A young cooartin' couple fro' Poon
Went under t'North Pier for a spoon.
Neaw t'wench 'uz towd t'lad
Uz 'e met bi a dad
Coz 'er's 'appen a bun in 'er oon.

A well-blessed young loony from Ozzy
Went swimmin' i't'cut beawt 'is cozzy.
'E said: "There's no 'arm
Advertisin' mi charm."
'E wozzn't so pots for rags, wozz 'e?

A Sundy Skoo teighcher fro' Skem
Were preawd 'e knowed aw abeawt Shem;
But sin 'e seed wenches
Sut cross-legged o't'benches
'E's wanntin' t'know aw abeawt them.

A bachelor tackler fro' Bowton
Once seed a wench sunbathe wi' nowt on.
'E said: "It's noan fair.
T'fust wench Ah've sin bare
Is t'sooart uz 'ad owt t'kept 'er cowt on."

Rhubarb

Mi faither used t'ave an allotment
As ned a big lot o'manure,
We ne'er 'ad no brass fo't'buy bag-muck
So we med do wi' scrawpin's off t'flooer.

Eawr milkmon an't'breadmon an't'muckmon
An't'paraffin feller o'course
An' 'im as fotched cockles an' mussels,
They aw 'ad a cart an' an 'orse.

So gerrin' manure were no bother
Whether it were dayleet or neet,
There were summat some gee-gee or other
'Ad just getten shut of i't'street.

I were eawt wi' mi bucket an' shovel
When a little wench wanntin' a chat
An' pintin' at wor I were shovellin'
Said: "Wor arta doin' wi' that?"

I said: "It's for purrin' o'rhubarb."
'Er said: "Theaw owt bi be'in' bars!
I reckon theaw'rt stark starin' ravin',
We allus 'ave custard on eawrs!"

Point of View

There were an owd geezer uz said to 'is wife
When 'e'd gi'ed t'Sunday papper a sken:
"Ah reckon uz everybody's quare bar us —
Un' theaw'rt quare neaw un' agen."

The Queen's English

When foreigners fail to fathom English
They fret the whole day long.
If both mean quite the opposite of right
Why doesn't left mean wrong?

They're baffled when they call at ten
To go with me to town.
My wife informs them I'm not up,
My son says I'm not down.

And if they know that P L O
And U G H spell plough
It's naughty then to giggle when
They call a cough a cow.

They're well aware both brace and pair
Can mean a tenth of a score
So why's a pair of braces not
A synonym of four?

We must explain again and again
Though some may call it treason
The Language of Our Gracious Queen
Has neither rhyme nor reason.

Communication

When I get most meticulous in my enunciation,
Particularly pernickety in my pronunciation,
My wife says ever so sweetly: "Joe, it's time to go, I think."
She knows I'll get the message that I've had enough to drink.

Titch

A-womm I were allus Titch
T'youngest o' four brothers
But though I ett mi pobbies
I never copped up t'others.

They were allus 'avin' me on,
They thowt they owt fer t'tease:
"Gi' o'er eightin' shortbread,
It's gi'in' thee duck's disease."

They said: "Fill thi clogs wi' 'orse-muck."
I feawnd it proper puzzlin'.
I really thowt I'd come to nowt
Unless I kept on guzzlin'.

They were aw as tall as tally-pows
On account of which
Because I favvered a dwarrf to them
They kept on cawin' me Titch.

I remember aw on us gooin'
Fer t' see eawr Aunt Matilda.
T'poor owd lass lived by 'ersen,
'Er'd noather mon nor childer.

My Mam 'ad made us goo;
Aunt Mattie was at death's dooer.
We never knowed worr ailed 'er
Burr it favvered there was no cure.

Though 'er knowed as 'er were deein'
Th'owd lass were proper brave.
'Er said: "I wannt yo' t'promise me
Yo'll carry me to mi grave."

We could do nowt else but promise,
'Er'd getten nob'dy else burr us,
Though we couldn't abide gooin' t' burryin's
An' cremations was a damn seet wuss.

⇨

Three on us was varnear skrikin'
Burr I couldn't say t'same fer eawr 'Ugh,
T'corner of 'is meawth kept twitchin',
'E favvered as 'e'd 'ad one or two.

We tip-toed eawt o't'room
Tryin' t' be as quiet as a meawse,
An' 'Ughie started chinkin'
As soon as we was eawt o' th' eawse.

'E said: "I cawn't 'elp lowfin'
Though 'appen we owt fer t' be worryin',
If we do what we promised eawr Auntie
It'll be a reet cock-up of a burryin'.

"Yon coffin is beawnd t' keck over,
It'll be a proper shambles then —
Three on us are mooer than six foot fooer
But Titch is nobbut five foot ten."

Talkin' Proper

Though 'ardly owt med Faither nowt
'E allus geet reet stroppy
If 'e copped aither Seth or me
Talkin' Lanky sloppy.

'E'd meck us stond i't'corner yon
Till we wuz wake at t'knees,
Sayin': "Ah went t't'tripe shop" till
'E 'eerd four separate T's.

Ah'm fain uz Ah were gradely towt,
Mi Dad were 'appen drastic,
Burr Ah con still seawnd separate T's
Wi' teeth wot's nobbut plastic.

The Test

They put mi into t'babbies' class
T'fust day I went t'skoo';
It favvered as they thowt I wuz
Nowt burr a slavverin' foo'.

So I upped an' axed t'Class Teighcher:
"Dost think as I'm an ass?
Mi mam's bin learnin' mi a-womm —
I owt t'be i't'fust class."

Wi went an' seed th'Ead-Mistress,
'Er said: "If theaw'rt a Throp
Babbies is t'reet class for thee —
Noan on yo's much cop.

"Burr I don't wannt t'upset thi
On thy fust day at t'skoo';
'Appen it's best fo't 'ave a test,
I'll see worr I con do."

So t'fust thing after playtime
I went i't'front o'th'Ead,
'Er said: "Aw t'Throps is strung i'th'arm
Burr allus wake i't'yed.

"Fo't see if theaw'rt a crate-egg
I'll nobbut ax one thing,
What comes after eight, nine, ten?"
An' I said: "Jack, queen, king."

I seed 'er sigh an' shake 'er yed,
Burr 'er voice were proper sweet
As 'er towd mi one of us 'ad t'bi wrung
An' it weren't me as were reet.

T'Pill

Yo'll 'ave 'eerd o'th'erb-mon, owd Bill Crank,
Uz studied 'Arry Stottle,
Worre'er it were uz were ailin' yer
'E'd meck yer up a bottle.

'E'd brimstone un' traycle fer warchin' guts,
'E'd senna tay fer t'mumps,
Un' 'is sawves un' eighls wuz beltin' fer beighls,
Carrybunkles un' gangreeny lumps.

Folk come fro' far uz weel uz near,
Fro' Skem un' Cocky Moor,
Un' i' Rodney Street they knowed aw reet
There were nowt uz Bill couldn't cure.

So when t'young wenches jacked 'im in
'E were gradely ta'en aback.
'E 'eerd they wuz feared uv 'avin' mooer kids
Un' thowt they owt 'ave a proper quack.

Th'owd 'erb-mon thowt if 'e didn't do nowt
'E'd leighze mooer'n 'afe 'is clients.
T'family planners wuz usin' scanners
Fer t'blind 'um aw wi' science.

Though 'Arry Stottle weren't no 'elp
It noan favvered t'bother owd Bill;
I' next to no time 'e knocked up
A contrairy-ceptive pill.

So t'wenches aw come flockin' back.
T'new pill sowd like 'ot cakes.
It favvered Bill 'ould 'appen afford
Fer t'go to Rhyl fer t'Wakes.

But then 'e were towed by a skrikin' wench:
"Ah've some road getten up t'stick
Though Ah've tecken t'contrairy-ceptive pill
Every neet for umpteen wick."

Bill said: "T'pill's noan fer teckin', lass.
So aw Ah con say's: 'Ard cheese!
Theaw owt t'ave read what t'label said:
'Owd tight between thi knees'!"

Name Game

Shakespeare said that if a rose
Were given a misnomer
It would when held beneath the nose
Emit the same aroma.

The use of euphemistic words
Makes simple things complex.
Why babble bosh about bees and birds
When what you mean is sex?

So surely we should all eschew
The latest aberration:
To give pretentious titles to
A person's occupation.

Even a menial manual task
Now has a nonsense name,
But you'll discover if you ask
The job is just the same.

Domiciliary Hygienicians
Have to work like skivvies;
Environmental Health Technicians
Have to empty privies.

If excavatory implements
Can be no better made
You'd think they'd use their commonsense
And call a spade a spade.

Fall from Grace

My grandad were a preighcher —
'E preighched at t'local Congs —
'E'd preighched at every chapel
Fro' Bickershaw to Bongs.

My fayther were a bolshie
As thowt religion dope
So I'd ne'er bin to t'chapel
Nor even t'Band of 'Ope.

We went to tay on Sundays,
We allus kept in touch,
But Grandad made it proper plain
I'd ne'er ameawnt to much.

I'd not bin browt up proper
So I'd 'ave for t'shape mysel',
If I wouldn't goo to t'Sunday Skoo'
I'd appen goo to 'Ell.

One day I felt fair clemmed —
Bally thowt my throat was cut.
So I pogged a shive o'bread
For t'ease my warchin' gut.

Bur I couldn't cod owd Grandad
An' while 'e were sayin' Grace
One eye skenned at t'bread-plate
An' t'other at t'crumbs on my face.

Though it's sixty year sin 'e said it
Yon Grace'll ne'er be forgetten:
"Thanks, Lord, for t'meight we're just beawnt eight
An' for yon eawr Jonty's etten."

A Joy for Ever

Of poets Keats may be the king
But he got it wrong, my boy.
It's a dirty mind, not a beautiful thing,
That brings everlasting joy.

Butties

We allus 'ad butties fer breakfast
Un' butties fer dinner uz weel;
A labourer's kids 'ad t'ayt butties —
'E'd no brass fer tripe ner keaw'eel.

We allus 'ad butties ut tay-time
Un' mooer afooer gerrin' i'bed;
Aw t'jackbit Mam managed t'ger 'owd on
It favvered we 'ad t'ave o' bread.

There wuz black traycle butties fer breakfast
Fer me un' eawr Eli un' Peg,
Burr if it were somebody's birthday
We'd 'appen get t'top off Dad's egg.

We'd chips on eawr butties fer dinner
Un' sugar o't'butties fer tay,
Though sometimes we geet Nestles' Milk on
When Dad 'ad some overtime pay.

There were nobbut marge on 'um at bedtime
But though we wuz stawdied wi' bread
Ah thowt there were nowt like a butty
Un' ne'er wannted owt else i'stead.

Dieticians met tell thi uz butties
Ne'er did nob'dy no good ut aw
Burr Ah'm in a seet bet-ther fettle
Than them uz is layin' deawn t'law.

Aw t'folk uz teck notice o' yon lot
Un' ayt nowt but yoggert un' such
'Ave noan getten t'bant o'weet lettuce —
It 'ould do 'um mooer good aytin' slutch.

They think uz we knowed nowt i't'twenties
When Ah were a skoo-lad i' clogs
But sin we gin o'er aytin' butties
This country's bin gooin' to t'dogs.

It's time someb'dy towd t'dieticians
Uz butties suit some folk a treat
Un' if we'd aw etten mooer butties
We met 'a' bin back on eawr feet!

Th'Alley Band (The Halle Orchestra!)

Aw t'family went to t'Free Trade 'Aw
When Fred fust fiddled fert th'Alley Band.
It were ram jam full fro' waw to waw
Bur aw t'folk favvered t'think Fred were grand.

When they'd 'eeard 'im plink-plonk t'pissycatty bits
They knowed t'reet road fert ax fer mooer:
While way sut in eawr seats like nits
They jumped up fert sheawt encooer.

Eawr Fred couldn't 'afe play yon veigholin —
Ah reckon 'e were bet-ther thun Rackymannyoff;
When 'e'd gi'ed um t'Bumble-bee they'd made that much din
Ah were feared t'bloody roof met a bin blowed off.

We aw went to t'do they 'ad afther t'show
Sin Fred 'ud wannted us t'meet 'is mates;
It cost us bugger-aw fert go —
It were aw bein' paid fer eawt o't'rates.

Fred's mates wuz jannock — proper jolly —
"We're good," they said: "But yore Fred's t'best!"
Un John Barbirolli said: "Fred were norra wally —
'E stood yed un showders o'er aw bloody rest."

Carry-on like yon ne'er bothered Fred —
'E didn't reckon much to such-like fuss;
Bur 'e knowed 'e'd bin damn good when Dad said:
"Ah dare say 'appen Ah met 'ave 'eeard wuss:
Aye Ah dare say 'appen Ah met 'ave 'eeard wuss!"

Owd Knowall

My Dad knowed aw th'owd sayin's
An' allus towd folk straight.
"What cawn't speighk cawn't lie," 'e'd say,
Or: "Them as doesn't work shouldn't eight."
"Theaw could meck a meal eawt o't'dish-clout."
'E'd say to a dab hand at cookin'.
Or: "Theaw weren't made at St. Helens, owd lad."
If theaw stood i't'road 'e were lookin'.

Worrever occurred 'e knowed t'reet word
But this is worr 'e towd me t'moost:
"There's plenty o'time for cooartin'
Afther t'pubs 'as loosed."
I believed worr 'e said an' ne'er geet wed
Till I were thirty-three.
"Them as weds young," 'e said, "rues lung."
An' I wouldn't lerr it 'appen to me.

Neaw aw o' my childer were wenches
So I ne'er gi'ed 'em Dad's advice.
"Grab t'fust mon," I said, "as axes you t'wed."
An' they ne'er ned tellin' twice.
My owdest lass were Jinny,
Another 'un as knowed it aw,
'Er Mam an' Dad met be noan so bad
Burr 'er Grandad druvv 'er up t'waw.

'Er were tellin' 'im 'eaw 'er were cooartin'
Wi' Toddy as towt at t'Tech
'E said: "If I were thee, owd love,
I'd gi'e yon crate-egg t'seck.
'E's nayther use nor ornament
An' 'is yed's full o' jolly robins,
'E goes to th'Allie beawt 'avin' no tay,
I reckon 'e's short o' bobbins."

"I know 'e's daft abeawt music," 'er said,
"I con see nowt wrung wi' that."
Dad towd 'er: "As per usual, lass,
Theaw'rt talkin' through thy 'at.
Theaw met 'ave umpteen GCE's
But theaw knows beggar aw abeawt life.
A mon as neglects 'is bally, owd love,
Allus neglects 'is wife."

Brid Wetchin'

I could wetch brids
Fro' morn till neet.
Throstles an' spadgers an' sheppies
Flittin' fro' branch to branch
Like Co-op managers,
Feightin' o'er crusses
Or pooin' wazzums eawt o't' greawnd,
Like tug o' warrs wi' 'lastic.
When I were a little lad
I thowt aw brids wuz black.
An' they were an' aw
Wi' t'smook fro' t'chimbleys.
But neaw it's like swoppin'
Your owd black an' white telly
For a spon-new colour set.
Throstles wi' breasts aw speckled
Like Sherlock 'Olmes's "band",
Spadgers not plain black
But breawn an' grey as weel,
An' sheppies aw t' colours o' t'rainbow,
Glitterin' like bits o' brokken glass
Reflectin' t' Blackpool leets.
It's another world.

Trams

Mi mam were noan a Leigther —
'Er come fro' Radcliffe road.
'Er'd nobbut two relations
Uz far uz Ah e'er knowed.

Their Mary Jane at Bury
Whose 'usband 'ad a farm;
Their Jem, a Farnworth baker,
Uz allus stunk o' barm.

So if we fancied seein'
Any kinfolk o' mi mam's,
It took aw day fo't' do it —
We 'ad t'go on eight trams.

Harry Barker 1984

If oather Bury or Farnworth
We 'ad t'go to un' from,
It took four trams fo't' teck us
Un' four fo't' fotch us womm.

We geet up breet un' early
Un' ett eawr egg un' beans,
Then took a South Lancs tramcar
Fro' Leighth to Four Lone Eends.

Past t'pit rucks un' th' owd tramshed,
'Owe Bridge un' Chowbent stations,
Un' then swopped to a tramcar
O' Bowton Corporation's.

Past Maggie Marshall's brew'eawse
Un' straight to Bowton then,
But when we geet t'Greight Moor Street
We 'ad t'swop trams agen.

We went part road to Bury
Wi' Bowton Corporation
Un' this time t'Coach un' 'Orses
Were t'tramcar's destination.

We clonked alung o't'tramlines
Wi't'driver clangin' t'bell
Un' gooin' uz fast uz leetnin'
Aw t'road to t'Coach 'Otel.

When mam 'ad med quite certain
We'd not come to no 'arm
A Bury Keawncil tramcar
'Ould teck us reet to t'farm.

Burr if it were i' Farnworth
Uz mam 'ad getten 'er date,
A different Bowton tramcar
'Ould teck us t'Moses Gate.

Un' when we landed yonder
We med eawr final swop
'Cause t'Farnworth Keawncil tramcar
Went reet past Uncle's shop.

Yo' folks uz nips to London
For a day eawt i' yer cars
Wain't credit uz yon one-way trip
'Ould 'appen teck three 'eawrs.

Bi t'time we'd 'ad eawr dinner,
Weshed up un' 'ad some tay,
Afore yo'd say Jack Robinson
We 'ad t'be on eawr way.

Dad liked us fo't' get womm
Afore t'Breawn Keaw chucked eawt
But t'trams took lunger still
T'go backerts road abeawt.

Eawr eawtin's favvered aw t'eend up
Wi feyther's blasts un' damns;
'E varnear allus missed 'is sup
When we'd bin on eight trams.

Although Ah've bin to th'eends o'th'earth
On trains un' planes un' ships
I reckon Ah've ne'er 'ad mooer fun
Than on yon tramcar trips.

Battle of the Bulge

If your work is classified as clerical
You mustn't fret or get yourself hysterical
Should you happen to find
Your exiguous behind
Showing startling signs of growing spherical.

For every sort of sedentary occupation
Can turn into a catch-22 situation,
Where every caloried crumb
Can bulge the belly or bum,
Producing plumpness in proliferation.

So, if your job necessitates some sitting
And you've got somewhat weighty quite unwitting,
You've got to stop the rot
Or else you'll go to pot
And need a lot of extra wool for knitting.

You need to be unshakably scientific,
Select a diet much less calorific.
Paradoxically when your bones
Have shed a couple of stones
The opposite sex will think you look terrific!

The Rat Race

The soul-destroying economic fight
Where no one cares as long as Jack's all right;
Where Ten Commandments seem to be forgot —
You mug your neighbour if you know what's what;
Where fortune favours liar, cheat and knave —
No wonder Queensberry's writhing in his grave;
And all to get that extra bit of cash
So wives may buy the more expensive trash.

The Joneses

Why try and keep up with the Joneses
To prove you've a five-figure income?
Why chatter on push-button phoneses
'Cause Jonesey considers they're dinkum?

Why try and keep up with the Joneses
To show you're not short of a bob?
Why splatter yourselves with Cologneses
'Cause Jonesey says they're just the job?

Why try and keep up with the Joneses
To tell us you haven't gone bust?
Why natter about precious stoneses
'Cause Jonesey insists they're a must.

Why flatter pestiferous Joneses
By doing the things that they do?
It's best to do things of your ownses
And let Jonesey keep up with you.

Peace Formula

The gentle sex,
Though easy to vex,
Is equally easy to please.
Just don't answer back
When they say white's black
Or chalk is synonymous with cheese.

To question the truth
Is utterly uncouth
When your wife's swears wrong is right.
You must be dense
If you haven't the sense
To answer: "Yes, dear. Quite!"

If at first . . .

Eawr Bob un' 'is missis Matilda
Wuz 'umpy uz sore-yedded bears
Because they'ad ne'er 'ad no childer
Although they'd bin wed twenty years.

One bedtime Matilda said: "Robert!
We'n booath on uz getten that crabby
We'll 'ave fo't do summat abeawt it
Afooer Ah'm too owd t'ave a babby.

"Ah reckon Ah've no chance o'kettlin'
Beawt teckin' advice from a quack.
T'morn neet when theaw gets womm fro't feawndry
We'll goo un' see owd Doctor Mac."

But when they'd towd t'quack aw abeawt it
Un' axed 'im fo't' gi' um a test
'E said: "Ah ne'er bother wi'yon lark,
Ah've allus thowt Nature knows best.

"There's nobbut one road t'meck a babby
So when yo' feel th'urge comin' on
Yo' moan't purr it off for a second,
Get crackin' uz quick uz yo' con.

"Yo'n no time t'goo upstairs to t'bedroom,
Yo'n no time for gerrin' undressed;
When t'pair on yo' start feelin' yon road
Reet theer un' reet then's allus t'best."

One mornin' a two-three wick later
Matilda said: "Bob! Ah feel sick.
Ah reckon theaw's managed fo't' crack it.
It favvers Ah'm 'appen up t'stick."

Uz soon uz 'is surgery oppened
'Er nipped for a check-up to t'quack
Un' said 'er were ever so grateful
Ut 'avin' bin purr o't'reet track.

Th'owd cock wuz uz chuffed uz Matilda,
'E said: "Ah knowed my road ud do it,
Ah 'ope uz you'll be very 'appy
Un wain't 'ave occasion fert rue it."

'Er said: "Ah cawn't wait t'be a mother.
Ah'm sick o'bein' nobbut a wife.
Burr 'appen it wain't aw bi wuth it —
We'n bin banned from Bingo for life."

Bully fer Me

Mi feyther cawed mi mam a foo';
'Er'd browt me up that mard
'E reckoned when Ah 'ad t'go t'skoo
Ah'd find it proper 'ard.

Burr Ah geet on aw reet at skoo
Though t'other lads wuz rough.
Life's nor allus aw up-broo
Fer them that's noan so tough.

Yon yobs uz 'appened t'try it on
Geet clog-marks on their bums
'Cause Ah sut next to Clogmon John
Un' 'elped 'im t'do 'is sums.

Clever Clogs

They said: "Yon's summat as cawn't be done."
I towd um: "There's nowt to it!"
I tackled yon job as couldn't be done
And I couldn't do it.

Deawn t'Yard

My Auntie allus towd me
I'd bin browt up reet marred.
'Er thowt as nowt bur a ta-ta
Were frittened o' gooin' deawn t'yard.

A-womm we 'ad a bath-room
Wi' a wesh-bow' and a loo,
And t'loo 'ad a seat beawt splinters
And a chain as yo' could poo'.

My Aunt's loo 'ad me 'eavin' —
'Er'd nor even getten a duckitt —
T'muck-mon cawed on a Setdy
And took it away in a bucket.

'Er'd getten no lavat'ry papper.
So what we 'ad for t'use,
'Ung up on a nail on t'petty waw,
Were last wick's Empire News.

I'll ne'er forget one day
At my Auntie's 'eawse at Shaw,
When I ran deawn t'yard to t'petty
There were nowt 'ung up on t'waw.

And bein' rayther in a rush
Wi' an 'eck of a warch i' my guts,
When I'd finished gerrin' shut
I used mi Comic Cuts.

I thowt I'd tell mi Auntie
Or 'er'd thowt me numb as a brick:
"We'n getten no papper i't'petty
And there's ne'er bin noan aw wick."

When I'd bin and gone and towd 'er
Mi lugs couldn't credit wor 'er said:
"t'petty met 'a' bin beawt papper,
But theaw's getten a tung i' thy yed!"

A Yank i' Lancs

My Uncle Tom were a cynic
As seldom oppened 'is gob;
'E lived near t'church at Winwick
Wheer 'e'd getten t'gravedigger's job.

One day 'e were weedin' t' garden
When 'e seed a Yank wi' a map,
And when 'e 'eerd "Beg pardon"
'E didn't oppen 'is trap.

'Cos Tom didn't 'owd wi' Yanks —
They'd aw getten too much chelp.
They ne'er said "Please" or "Thanks",
So Tom ne'er gi' 'em no 'elp.

But t' Yankee didn't tack th' 'uff —
'E mun 'a' thowt Tom stone-jug —
And although 'e were eawt o' puff
'E bawled deawn Tom's reet lug.

And when 'e'd done wi' sheawtin'
Tom knowed what was wrung aw reet:
'E were on a seet-seein' eawtin'
And 'e'd seen nobbut even one seet.

'E'd skenned every nook i' Winwick
Fro' Croft to Burtonwood,
'E'd bin to t' loony bin and t' clinic
An' fun' noan of it no good.

'E'd bin to t' village bobby,
'E'd axed a mon on t' bus,
'E'd axed i' t' Swan's back lobby
But nobody knowed wheer they wuz.

So afore 'e went back womm
'E were 'avin' one last try;
So 'e said to Uncle Tom:
"You look an intelligent guy.

"Does nobody know St. Oswald's Well?
Somebody must know, surely."
But Tom said: "Nay, lad, t' truth for t' tell
I didn't even know 'e'd bin poorly!"

Wrostlin'

Mi youngest brother Abel
'E varnear never spook;
'E ne'er favvered t'ear nowt noather —
'E'd allus 'is yed in a book.

'E learnt that much wi readin'
'E geet a prize at skoo',
A book wi' umpteen things in
Uz 'andy lads could do.

'E gi'ed o'er gooin' eawt playin'
Wi' t'other little lads
Un' started t'meck a spyglass
Fro' some owd specs o' Dad's.

Un' when 'e'd bin un' med it
'E'd sit upstairs for 'eawrs.
But Dad said uz 'e'd cop no 'arm
Just sut theer wetchin' t'stars.

Ah reckon Dad were mistecken —
That's why 'e geet a shock
When Abe come deawn for supper
One neet at nine o'clock.

Eawr kid said: "Yon young couple
Uz lives o'er t'shop's noan reet.
They wrostle bare i't'bedroom
T'best part of every neet."

A Rum 'Un

T' wife's a little rum 'un
Though 'er favvers proper un' prim.
Yo've 'appen ne'er 'eeard o't'parson
Un' t'trick 'er played on 'im.

Not lung afore Ah met 'er
'Er were wi' 'er mate i'Wales,
Wheer booath on um bowt bikinis
I't th' eend o't'season sales.

Bikinis then were darin',
Reawnd theer they wu'n't i'fashion;
I' Rhyl they still wuz wearin'
Yon kecks uz kills yo'r passion.

T'wenches thowt it better
T'goo on a quiet beach,
So bein' th'eend o'season
They'd nobbut far fo't'seech.

They'd stripped deawn to t'bikinis
Un'lay stretched eawt o't'sonds
When up come a po-faced parson
Wi' a towel in 'is 'onds.

Un' when 'e seed yon wenches
Showin' varneer aw they'd geet
'E stopped un' started sheawtin'
Like a mon uz 'ad gone noan reet.

"We wannt no naked Jezebels
Gi'in' dacent church folk shocks.
Wenches wi' bare bally buttons
Owt t'bi purr i't'stocks."

While t'wife were wonderin' what fo't' do
T'gerr even wi'th'owd cock
'E walked to t'other eend o't'beach
Un' went be'ind a rock.

But when 'e swum reet eawt o'seet
They went fo't 'ave a toot
Then t'wife took 'er bikini off
Un' stood in 'er birthday suit.

'Er said: "Ah'll larn yon mon
  t'think twice
Afore 'e oppens 'is trap;
'E's 'id a camera in 'is clooas,
Pick it up un' teck a snap."

T'photo ta'en un' clooas back on
Yon wenches ran like 'ell,
Lowfin' like 'yenas
Aw t'road to their 'otel.

Because they reckoned it likely,
Rayther than nobbut just p'raps,
Uz one on 'is congregation
'Ould 'appen develop 'is snaps.

Un' 'e 'ould tell t'Church Keawncil
Uz t'mon they thowt a prude
'Ad spent a wick's retreat i'Wales
Snappin' tarts i't'nude.

Thwarted

I planned my kids' careers with care —
My first-born's a physician;
My youngest girl's a pharmacist,
The other's an optician.
My son's a dental surgeon, so
It isn't hard to guess
The purpose of my planning was
My private NHS.
But, as Burns said, the best-laid plans
Are apt to gang agley.
The nearest of my offspring lives
Two hundred miles away.

T'Local Rag

Mi faither's eighty-fooar
An' 'e'll do a scooar mooar;
'E'll live t' be an 'undred aw reet.
'E's getten fawed arches
An' aw sooarts o' warches,
An' th' eye-staggy's teckin' 'is seet.

'E ne'er goes eawt,
Just lozzes abeawt,
Skennin' at t'local rag,
An', w'en I've seen
'Im screw 'is een,
I've chunnered bur 'e sez: "Don't nag."

"I'm nor a whipper-snapper,
So ger it i' thi napper,
If I cawn't 'ave t'papper, I'll fret.
I 'ave fo't'read,
'Cause I wou'n't know I'd deed
Till I seed it i'th'Gazette."

T'Fust Fawin' Eawt

Mi missus fust fawed eawt wi' me
T'day afther we wuz wed;
When we'd walked past a bonny 'en
Ah'd 'appened t'turn mi yed.

Ah said: "Yon's nowt fo't' fret abeawt.
It's t'road men's made, dost see?
When Ah waint wannt t'wetch aw t'other tarts
Ah waint 'ave t'bant t'wannt thee!"

T' Naked Truth

When t'Mensa champ
Went t'Nudist Camp
Fo't'teck 'is I.Q. test
They said: "Wait theer
Just sut i't'cheer
Until we'n getten undressed.

"Neaw this is t'job:
Don't oppen thi gob
But sooart us into classes."
"Aw reet!" t'champ said
"Ah'll do it on mi yed
When Ah've bin un' fotched mi glasses."

'E knowed for sure
When 'e walked through t'dooer,
Not bein' doolally nor numb,
A workin' mon's
Getten segs o'th' onds,
A boss 'as segs o't'bum.

T' Warrnin'

Mi Mam were allus warrnin' me:
"Ne'er wed a pratty nowt
Or every eawnce of 'appiness
Is beawnt be dearly bowt".

"Thee teck no notice!" said mi Dad.
"Ne'er mind 'er. T'truth fo't'tell,
Ah reckon Ah've done noan so bad;
Un Ah wed one mi-sel'."

Neighbours

Ah thowt when we fust come fo't'live 'ere
Worr a champion place we wuz at;
Aw t'neighbours 'ad names uz wuz Lanky
Like Ramsbottom, Ogden un' Platt.

We'd Butterworths, Haworths un' Unsworths,
Duckworths un' Shuttleworths too,
Greenhalghes, Greenoughs un' Faircloughs,
Uz Lanky us sayin': "Eaw do!"

We'd Alcocks un' Wilcocks un' Silcocks,
Adcocks un' Pidcocks uz weel,
Culshaws un' Forshaws un' Kershaws,
Uz Lanky uz tripe un' keaw 'eel.

There met 'a'bin one or two Murphies
Un' 'appen a Jones or McGraw,
But neaw there's that many folk flitted
We'n noan o'th'owd neighbours ut aw.

We cawn't sterr for Khans un' Gorkinskis,
Patels un' Corellis un' Singhs,
Un' names uz seawnd deawnreet doolally,
Keeyeekees un' Gumboos un' Yings.

Ut fust Ah just couldn't teck to 'um,
They favvered a quare sooart o'folk.
They couldn't meck nowt o'mi Lanky,
Ah couldn't tell one word they spoke.

But sin' they'n bin reawnd 'ere for ages
Ah've getten fo't'know a good few.
Their childer's bin browt up reet gradely
Un' learnt fo't talk proper ut t'skoo.

They'n tecken a while fo't' get used to
But neaw there's no bother nor fuss.
We gerr on aw reet wi't'new neighbours
Un' they favver t'gerr on wi' us.

But t'Fascists keep breighkin' their windows;
T'daft beggars owt t'leighve 'um a-be,
There's nowt wrung wi' t'young Yings un' Gumboos —
They speighk bet-ther Lanky ner me!

T'Corner Shop

I remember gooin' errands
To Shufflebottom's shop,
Fotchin' bread or pratoes
Or 'appen a bottle o' pop.

One day we'd getten no traycle
So I went reawnd theer wi't'jug;
I remember owd Shuffy turnin' t' tap
And it comin' eawt glug-glug-glug.

Then 'e put t' jug deawn o' t' keawnter
And said: "Neaw! Wheer's thy brass?"
And I felt my lugs go red as fire
'Cos I knowed as I'd been an ass.

I'll allus remember Shuffy.
I'll ne'er forgerr 'is mug
When I said: "I've dropped a clanger,
T'brass is at t' bottom o' t' jug."

Dad's Advice

A wench owt t' allus wed for love,
'Er ne'er owt t' wed for brass,
But faw i' love wi' t' gaffer's lad
And theaw wain't go wrung, owd lass!

T'Monkey Run

I remember when there was Monkey Runs
Wheer t'lasses an' t'lads used t'meet;
Leigh's were allus Railway Road
An' Bongs'iz Elliott Street.
On a Setday neet, whether dry or weet,
We allus went Up Leigh
An' t'neighbours knowed it were Railway Road
For my mate 'Arry an' me.

We thrutched along i't'thick o't'throng,
It were mooer a scrum than a stroll,
We mooched along to t'Turnpike, then
Mooched aw t'road back to t'Dole.
We 'ad no brass for t'teck a lass
I'th'ale'eawse for a sup,
So t'lads kept trapesin' up an' deawn
An' t'lasses deawn an' up.

Every wench as wannted t'wed
Went walkin' every wick
Lookin' for a likely lad
An' 'opin' as they'd click.
'T were th'only road for t'meet a mon
As 'ould 'appen ax 'er t'marry,
Burr 'Eaven 'elp t'tart as set 'er 'eart
On me or my mate 'Arry.

We'd both bin browt up proper like
Wi' 'ugs an' kisses an' clouts,
Burr I allus reckon it moan't 'a' tecken —
We was nobbut a pair o' nowts.
We'd ne'er two 'awpneys t'rub t'gether
For buyin' fleawrs or lockets,
If we'd getten a couple o' thrippney joes
They brunt 'oles in eawr pockets.

Eawr brass aw went on coffin-nails
Or were spent wi' a bookie's runner,
It were no life for t'share wi' a wife
Especially one as 'ould chunner.
But God 'as getten funny roads
O' bringin' things to pass,
An' one fine neet 'E geet things reet;
I fawed i' love wi' a lass.

It were love at fust seet, I loved aw as 'er'd geet,
An' I went as wake as a kitten,
Burr I'd 'ardly winked when my arm were linked
An' I knowed as 'er were smitten.
It were gerrin' dark, it were miles to t'Park,
So we went at t'back o't'Congs,
An' 'er towd me theer 'er name were Leah
An' 'er'd come o't'tram fro' Bongs.

An' then 'er said 'er wannted t'wed
A rayther special chap,
Six foot two wi' eyes o'blue
Wi' summat under 'is cap.
'Er'd seeched 'ere, theer an' everywheer
Burr 'er plan 'ad bin banjoed,
There were nob'dy reet in Elliott Street
So 'er'd come for t'try Railway Road.

'Er said I'd do though my eyes wasn't blue
An' I were nobbut five foot nine;
If I'd jack in t'fags an'backin't'nags
An' use my yed 'er were mine.
Neaw Leah an' me are at t'top o't'tree,
I'm a Mester J'iner an'Builder
Wi' lovin' pride i'my bonny Bongs bride
An' seven champion childer.

I never thowt I'd ameawnt to owt
But neaw I'm even o't'Bench
An' aw because my missus was
A gradely Lancashire wench.
It's quare 'eaw wives con change eawr lives
'Cause when aw's said an' done
I'd ne'er be wheer I am if Leah
'Adn't swopped 'er Monkey Run.

Th'en Pen

Sin' 'im un' Mam loved chucky eggs
Un' so did me un' 'Ettie
Dad thowt 'e met uz weel keep 'ens
So 'e med a pen near t'petty.

T'fust day 'e dished eawt th'Indycorn
Uz jackbit fer 'is pullets
Throstles, sheppies un' spadgers come
Un' golloped it deawn their gullets.

While Dad were sheawtin': "Bugger off!"
Un' cloddin' bricks at t'brids,
T'parson fro'next dooer cawed eawt:
"Gi'e o'er cussin' i' front o't'kids!

"A mon uz'll cuss when childer's theer
Owt t'ang 'is yed i'shame.
Aw theaw 'as t'do is sheawt eawt: 'Shoo!'
Un' t'brids'll bugger off just t'same."

Clanger

When Sam were cooartin' Lizzie Ann
'E took 'er o't'North Pier
Fo't' 'eark at Wingates Temperance Band
Uz 'appened fo't'bi theer.

But sin' Sam nobbut knowed one tune
Uz 'e cawed t'Peasant un' t'Poet
'E felt fair flummoxed when 'er said:
"What's yon they're playin'? Dost know it?"

Just then 'e skenned a Notice Booard
Reet near wheer they were sittin',
Un' said: "It favvers, Lizzie love,
It's cawed: 'Refrain from Spittin'."

What Santa Fotched

Mi brother were nowt bur a nowt,
'E allus kep' gerrin' i'bother;
It favvered 'e couldn't do owt
Beawt gerrin' o't'wrung side o'Mother.

'Er ne'er left 'im lung beawt a clout,
'Er clattered 'is lugs an' 'is bum;
Bur 'e wouldn't gi' o'er bein' nowt —
I reckon 'e mun 'a'bin numb.

Mi Mother were at 'er wits' eend,
An' one neet 'er said to mi Dad:
"It favvers theaw's faithered a fiend
As is 'ell-bent on gooin' to t'bad.

"I reckon 'is rump's med o' wood
An' 'e's getten a cast-iron yed,
Chastisin' 'im's doin' no good
An' I cawn't think of owt else i'stead."

Mi Dad weren't a dab 'and at thinkin',
'E were mooer for 'is bacca an' beer,
Bur in between smookin' an' drinkin'
'E thowt up a beltin' idea.

"If it 'as fo't bi summat reet shockin'
I reckon there's nobbut one cure;
When 'e 'angs up 'is Christmas Eve stockin'
I'll fill it to t'top wi' manure."

When flatrib were two pints to t'shillin'
There wuz plenty of 'orses o't'street
So Dad 'ad no bother i'fillin'
Seth's stockin' wi' orse-muck that neet.

Next morning eawr kid geet up early
Fo't'see wor owd Santa 'ad left.
Wor 'e said varnear turned mi yure curly,
'E were cussin' like someb'dy bereft.

I cawn't abide owt as is coarse
So I axed 'im t'gi o'er carryin' on.
'E said: "T'crate-egg fotched mi an 'orse
Bur 'e ne'er teed it up so it's gone!"

Mother's Pledge

They med mi mother teck a pledge
When'er were nobbut nine:
Nob'dy's lips uz touch strung drink
'Ull e'er bi touched bi mine."

Mi faither ne'er were eawt o't'pub,
'E loved 'is bottled beer;
But Mother ne'er 'ad t'breighk 'er pledge,
'E kept 'er conscience clear.

Because when Faither 'ad a sup
'E'd teck it straight fro't'bottle;
'E reckoned t'waste noan on 'is lips,
It aw went deawn 'is throttle.

Welcome?

I't'warr Ah were a sowjer
Un' when Ah went on leave
Gradely Lanky welcomes
Allus med me grieve.

When Ah landed womm o't'dar-step
Wi' mi kitbag un' mi pack
It weren't: "Eaw lung 'as t'come fer?"
But: "When art gooin' back?"

T'Good Owd Days

Mi greight-grandad 'ates modern ways,
'E's allus gooin' on abeawt t'good owd days
An' worr a beltin' time they 'ad
Afooer owd England went to t'bad.
I reckon 'e's Lancashire's champion forgetter,
Things wuz different then, not better.

At t'Derby match when t'Blues byitt t'Reds
They met norr a clouted one another's yeds
Or fowt wi' bicycle chains an' knives,
But they aw went womm an' clogged their wives.
There wuz 'appen no footbaw 'ooligans but
Refs kept gerrin' chucked i't'cut.

'E sez it were greight fo't'be alive
When Woodies wuz two owd pence for five,
Burr 'e ne'er lets on as when 'e 'ad a job
'E worked aw wick for thirty-five bob.
An' they'd purr 'im o't' parish for a couple o' wicks
If 'e didn't clock on o't'dot o'six.

'E reckons folk don't know 'eaw fo't'eight,
It's aw yon jazzed-up packet meight.
No wonder aw t'young women's thin,
Aw they can do is oppen a tin!
Burr 'e were skin an'bone when 'e were a lad
'Cause bread an' scrape were aw 'e e'er 'ad.

'E carries on abeawt 'eaw things are
Burr 'e ne'er sez nowt abeawt t'fust world warr;
A bob a day were not so much
For four year up to t'knees i'slutch.
'E's waitin' fo't' "Land Fit for 'Eroes" yet,
It's 'appen as weel owd men forget.

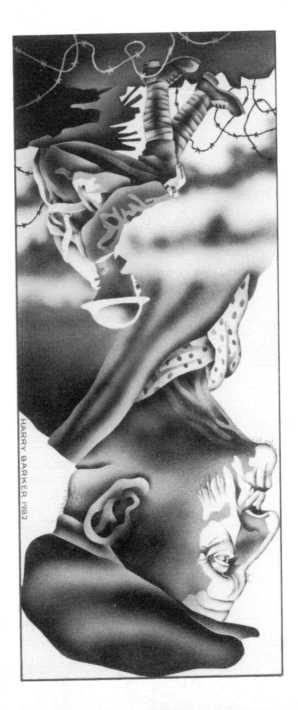

T'Census

T'other wick when they took t'census
An' I met t'census mon
Mi memory took mi back a bit
To Nineteen Forty One.

I were teckin' t'census then misel'
In a place cawed Chequerbent
An' I varnear jacked mi job in theer
At t'fust 'eawse wheer I went.

A dear owd lady oppened t'dooer,
T'dead spit o' mi Granny,
'Er said: "Worrever theaw'rt sellin', cock,
I wain't bi wanntin' anny."

But when I towd 'er 'oo I were,
I 'ave fo't' gi' 'er credit,
'Er took in every word I said
Varneear afooer I'd said it.

An' when I'd tecken 'er particlers deawn
I said: "Reet, Mrs. Grundy,
I'll caw back for thi' Census Form
A wick this comin' Monday."

I dursn't write deawn worr I thowt,
'Cause nobody 'ould print it,
When 'er said: "I don't know what theaw means,
Today is Monday, i'n't it?"

'Er gradely geet mi meighthered then,
I said: "Nay, Missus, nay!
I reckon theaw's getten thi days mixed up,
It's nobbut Setd'y today."

We argued t'toss for o'er an 'eawr
Until th'owd lass said: 'Sithee!
I'm *tellin'* thi as it's Monday neaw,
I'm norr arguin' wi' thi!"

Bi this time I were pow-fagged,
Not to mention vexed,
I'd getten a splittin' yed-warch
An' I didn't know what t' do next.

Then aw of a sudden fro' nowheer
These words come into mi yed:
"Ne'er mind abeawt a wick next Monday,
I'll caw a wick on We'n'sd'y instead!"

Feeshin'

Them as feesh mun bi noan reet,
They're aw as nutty as slack.
They start t'fust thing an' feesh till neet
An' then they clod 'um aw back.

But they're noan as numb as t' missus's dad —
'E's gradely off 'is yed —
'E reckons as feeshin's flamin' mad
So 'e wetches 'um feesh instead!

Utter Snobbery

Whenever I take flowers to Ma's
She says: "I'll put them in a vahze."
If I take a bunch to Mother-in-Law's
She says: "I'll put them in a vawze."
But both mums gaze in shocked amaze
If someone says: I'll purr 'em in a vaize."

Hangover

I wouldn't be in the state I'm in
Nor would I feel so chronic
If I'd gone easy with the gin
Instead of with the tonic.

Harry Barker '84